TO BOOK THE FOOD INTELLIGENCE ONLINE PROGRAMME

To use this book successfully, we recommend that you purchase the Food Intelligence Online Course which is used in conjunction with this book. Please go to, admin@fullpotentialtraining.com.au to purchase the course. Both the book and online course are ideal for School, Group and Holiday Programmes.

OBJECTIVE AND OUTCOME FOR THE YOUNG ADULT

OBJECTIVE Meeting: SCOOTLE TLF ID M016338

By the end of this short course, you will understand how to identify the role the molecule plays in the food you eat, how processed sugar and trans-fat can add to ill health, and how food additives are now put into more than 10,000 bought foods worldwide and their negative effects on global, human health.

OUTCOME

You will be able to make beneficial, good food choices that help your body to grow, stay healthy, and can work towards your goals in learning and education; you will think before you take the first bite and will have the knowledge to make other healthy food choices.

For teachers and programme providers, please see Meeting Curriculum Objectives, Nutrition Page 54.

If you have purchased this book without its cover, it may be a stolen book.
Neither the publisher or the author is under any obligation to provide professional services in anyway, legal, health or in any form which is related to this book, its contents advice or otherwise.

The law and practices vary from country to country and state to state. If legal or professional information is required, the purchaser, or the reader should seek the information privately and best suited to their particular needs and circumstances.
The author and publisher specifically disclaim any liability that may be incurred from the information within this book.
All rights reserved.
No part of this book, including the interior design, images, cover design, diagrams, or any intellectual property (IP), icons and photographs may be reproduced or transmitted in any form by any means (electronic, photocopying, recording or otherwise) without the prior permission of the publisher. ©

Copyright© 2022 MSI Australia
All rights reserved.

Published by How2Books
Under licence from MSI Ltd, Australia
Company Registration No: 642923859
NSW, Australia
See our website: www.how2books.com.au
Or contact by email: admin@booksforreadingonline.com
Covers and Copyright owned by MSI, Australia

MSI acknowledges the author and images used in this book.

ISBN: 978-0-6451612-6-7

Working together to create a sustainable world

TOPICS

- Looking at the food you eat
- The journey of the molecule
- Palm oil
- The state of the arteries
- The devil of sugar
- Defining carbohydrates
- Understanding sweeteners
- Brain hunger
- Symbiotic relationships
- The magical story of the key and the lock
- Green and leaf vegetables
- Food additives
- The story of caffeine
- Your immune system
- The paradox of the situation – palm oil
- Marketing
- For teachers and programme providers

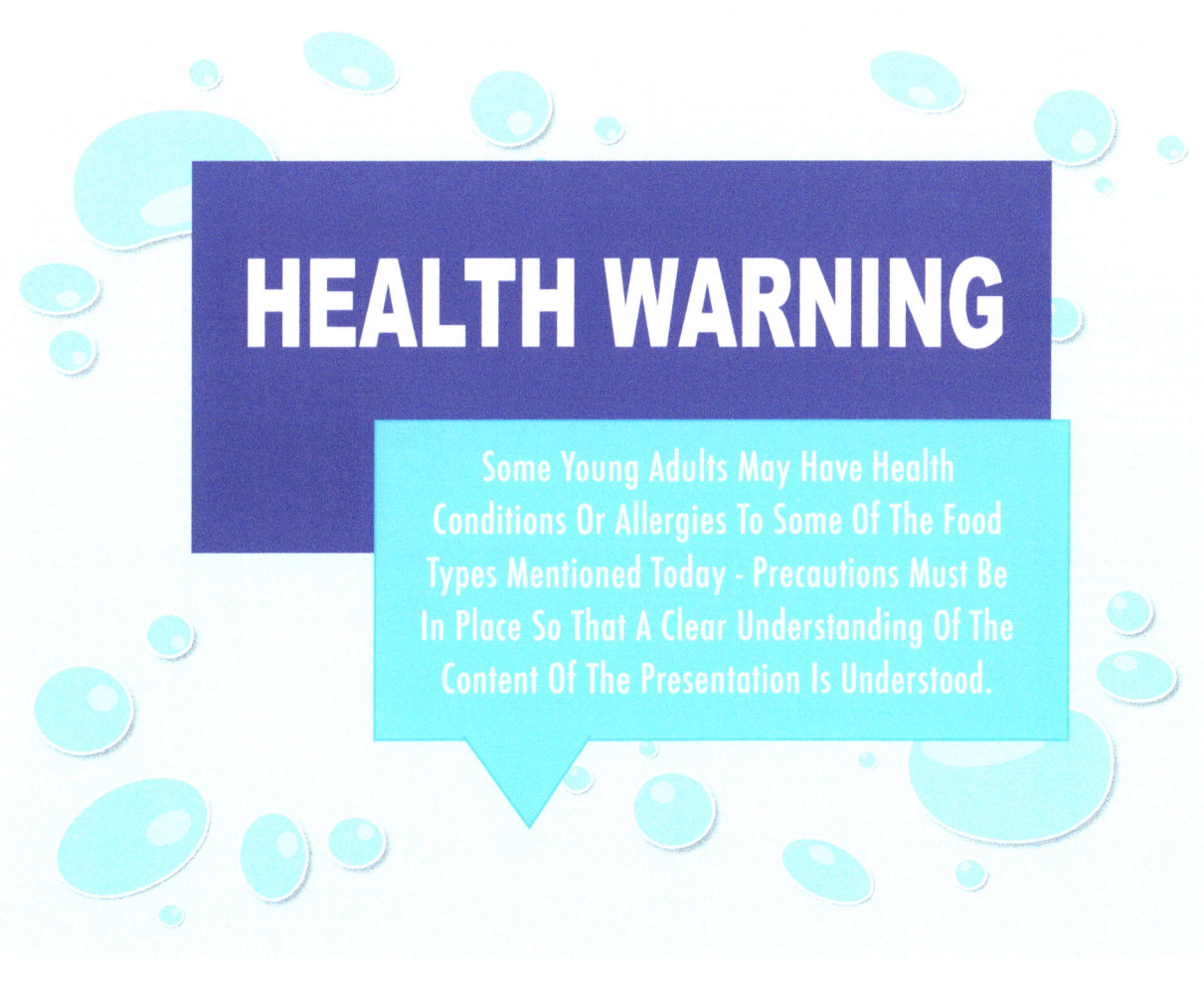

LOOKING AT THE FOOD YOU EAT

The original word food may have come from the word: fode or fude (Middle English) from foda (Old English or from fodo (Proto Germanic)[1]. Regardless of the word origin, food is meant to keep us healthy. In the last 200 years, food has done far from that.

We are now in the 21st Century and we are still recovering, food wise, from the Industrial Revolution that began in the 18th Century. As small agricultural societies became more industrialised and small communities moved into the towns and cities; this was especially so in England and parts of Great Britain. The Industrial Revolution provided work for the masses and food was needed to keep the masses working in the newly developed factories and sweat shops; these establishments later stretched into other parts of the world.

To feed the masses and to keep the price affordable so that factory workers and their families could be fed, mechanism and machinery took over the production of food.

In the 21st century, working through a pandemic, which the origins may be food related, and we are still learning about the food we should or should not eat!

Your food is the petrol in your tank; if you put dirty, cheap, or unusable fuel (food) in your tank, you will not go anywhere; you will become stationary. If you continue to do this deed throughout life, you will see the consequences in ill health.

Your food journey is a fascinating journey, so let's enjoy that journey together by starting with talking about molecules.

---
[1] https://www.quora.com.

THE JOURNEY OF THE MOLECULE

So, what is a molecule? Molecules are contained within the food we eat and the drink we drink; molecules are also in the air we breathe. To keep it simple and for our purposes, a molecule has a fatty glycerol head and three legs consisting of hydrogen and carbon, these are called chains. Within food processing the molecule can be changed through hydrogenation, this is a process of heating, usually with food oils, to create a reaction between the hydrogen and carbon chain. A catalyst such as nickel, palladium or platinum rods are used to create molecular changes to the molecule.

From now on, we will use symbols to identify the healthy and unhealthy molecules; the green tick representing healthy molecules and food, and the grey cross, identifying unhealthy molecules and unhealthy food.

On the next page, in healthy fat, shows a natural molecule with three healthy legs, attached to a glycerol head. Each leg, as I have said previously, contains a hydrogen and carbon chain. Such a molecule is known as a healthy, unsaturated fat.

When each leg of the chain is free and lose it has mobility and movement; this type of molecule is good to have within our food because it is recognised as it passes on its journey from the mouth and through the body's digestive system.

HEALTHY MOLECULE SHOWING THREE, FREE-FLOWING HYDROGEN AND CARBON LEGS

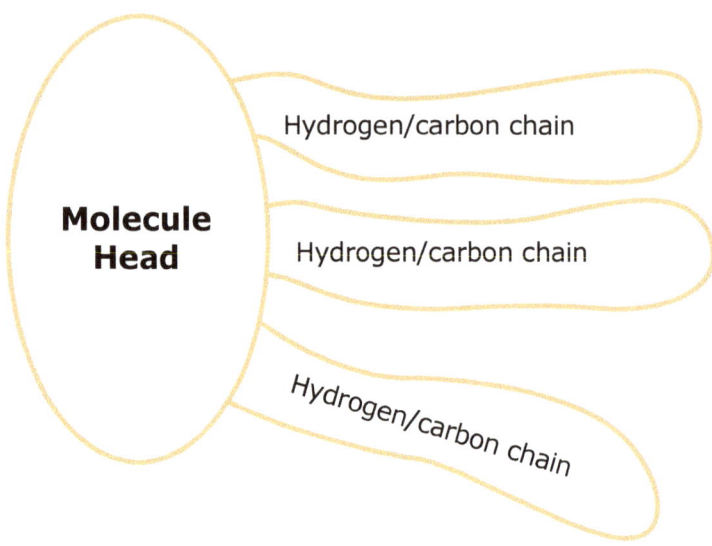

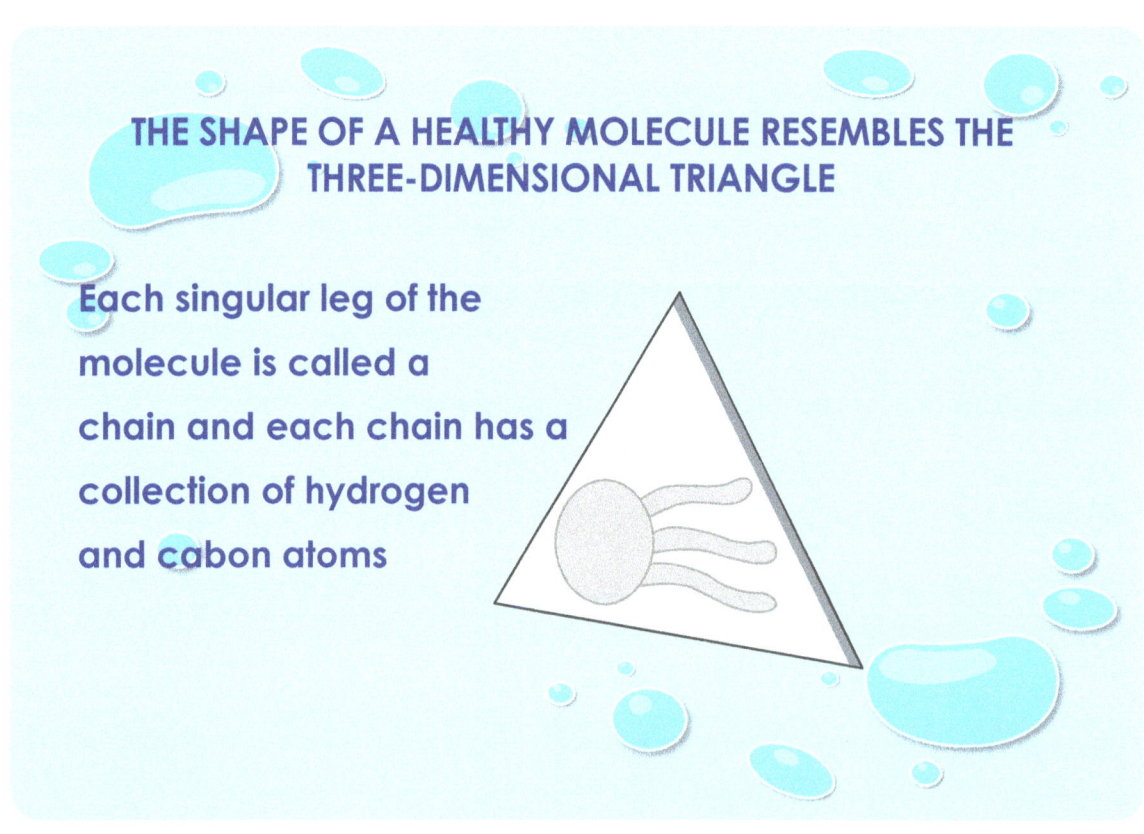

HEALTHY MOLECULES ARE WITHIN FRESH FRUIT AND VEGETABLES

Because molecules are small, they cannot be seen with the naked eye. Within 25mm, 100,000,000 molecules are within that measurement. Now let's gain an understanding of the size of molecules within a bite of a fresh banana. Each 25mm bite of a fresh banana will have an estimated 100,000,000 healthy molecules.

Question: When was the last time you ate a piece of fresh fruit?

Your Answer: ……………………………………………………………………………………

YOUR NOTES

……
……
……
……
……
……
……

MOVING ON FROM THE BANANA

Looking at the journey of an egg sandwich, how many of you have had an egg sandwich recently...?

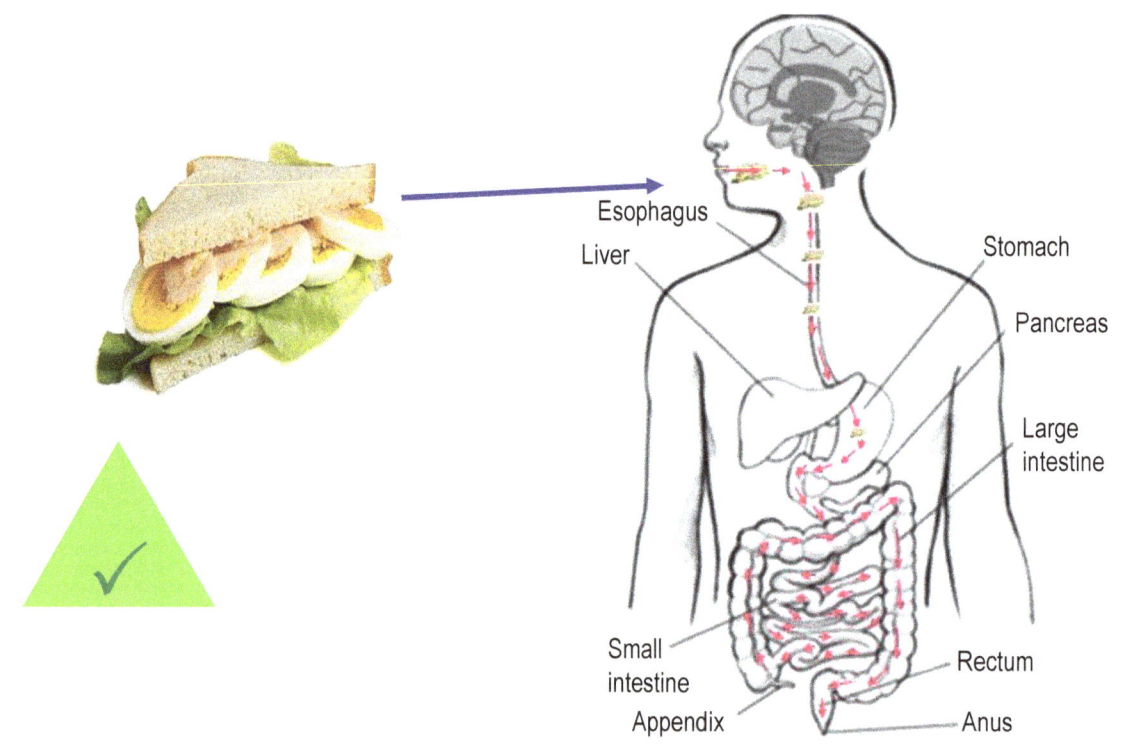

EATING HEALTHY FOOD WITH HEALTHY MOLECULES

To start eating an egg sandwich, first, you need to take a bite and chew the contents of the sandwich. The contents are swallowed and then go from the mouth, down the esophagus, into the stomach where the stomach acids take over and start to break down the content of the sandwich.

While passing through the stomach, both the pancreas and liver release enzymes that further help to breakdown fats and sugars of the food.

From the stomach, the macerated food will move into the small intestine where the intestine will involuntarily squeeze the remaining food; this contains the goodness of the food including vitamins and minerals, in the form of molecules. The squeezing of the intestine allows the extracted molecules, to penetrate the intestinal wall and go into the bloodstream.

We have just spoken about healthy molecules but there are unhealthy molecules in many of the foods we buy and eat. These unhealthy molecules are not recognised by the enzymes in your gut, these are known as empty or dead molecules.

SO, WHAT IS AN EMPTY AND DEAD MOLECULE?

As I have previously mentioned, hydrogenation is a heating process that changes the healthy molecule makeup into a dead or empty molecule makeup; these changed molecules are now put into everyday foods sold worldwide and are in the food distribution chain.

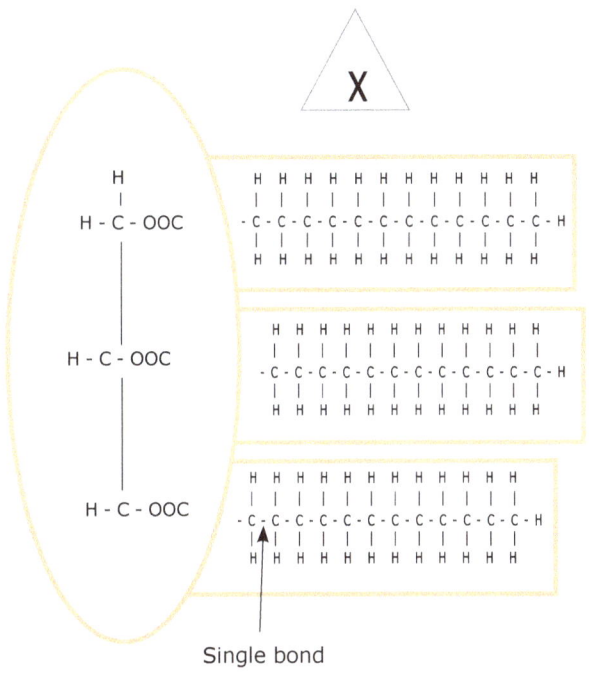

Through the hydrogenation process, the molecules within fats such as cooking oils, will go from an unsaturated fat to a saturated fat. As can be seen opposite, and unlike the unsaturated fat molecule, saturated fat molecules have hard, straight legs. Saturated fats are used in everyday eaten foods worldwide.

Please refer to the molecule free-moving legs on page 4.

Once a fat is changed from an unsaturated fat to a saturated fat, it then comes under the heading of **TRANS-FAT.**

PALM OIL

Palm oil in its natural form may have health benefits. However, to make it ready for use in the fast-food industries, this oil also goes through the hydrogenation process converting the healthy molecules to unhealthy trans-fat molecules which make it a saturated fat. This makes it unacceptable to the human gut and adds to ill health through building cholesterol in your arteries.

Samples of Trans-fat foods

- Doughnuts
- Biscuits
- Baked cakes, some breads and bread rolls such as brioche
- Cakes of all types
- Desserts
- Chocolates
- Ready for use frozen pastry and pastry products
- Potato chips and crisps
- Many varieties of corn chips and other like foods
- A range of widely used cooking oils used in the fast-food take away food industries
- Margarines and some butter
- Frozen and pre-cooked baked dinners and other pre-cooked meals.

THE ADVANTAGES TO THE FAST-FOOD INDUSTRY USING SATURATED FATS IN COOKING OILS

- Oils last longer and do not need changing as often after cooking, therefore the cost of cooking oil is greatly reduced
- Larger quantities of food can be cooked in the same batch
- Saturated fats can be used in a large range of foods including the bakery, chocolate, and butter industries. Saturated fats (trans-fats) are used in many industries as mentioned. However, in the butter

industry, a saturated fat allows butter, margarine, and other spreads to remain solid, which allows them to be used for spreading as in bread and butter. When saturated fat is used in chocolate making, it allows the chocolate to be used in confectionary.

Can you last recall when you ate a cream doughnut………………………………………………………………..?
Day……………………………………………………………………………?
Knowing it is made with saturated fat, would you eat it again……………………………………………………………………..?

When did you last eat a ham or beef burger…………….?
Day……………………………………………………………………………?
Knowing it is made with saturated fat, would you eat it again………………………………………………………………………?

When did you last eat chocolates …………………………..?
Day……………………………………………………………………………..?
Knowing it is made with saturated fat, would you eat it again……………………………………………………………………….?

YOUR NOTES

……
……
……
……

SO, WHAT IF YOU EAT SATURATED FAT FOODS OVER A LONG PERIOD OF TIME?

The answer is simple, saturated fat clogs arteries and makes you unwell; maintaining an unhealthy diet leads to ill-health.

THE STATE OF ARTERIES

The state of a healthy artery

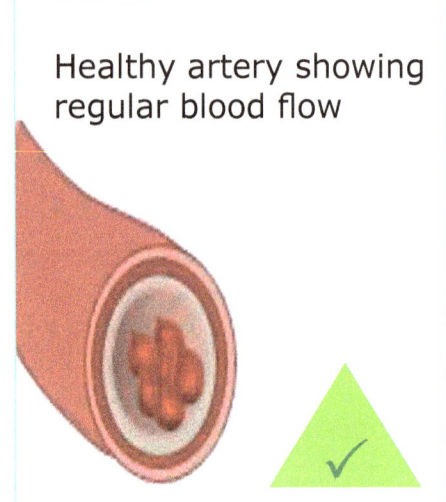

Healthy artery showing regular blood flow

With healthy arteries, the blood flow travels easily around your body.

If you have a habit of eating unhealthy food, from the age of twenty years old, cholesterol will start to build up in the artery walls within your body.

The state of an unhealthy artery

When cholesterol starts to build up in the arteries, you will start to feel breathless and have other health problems.

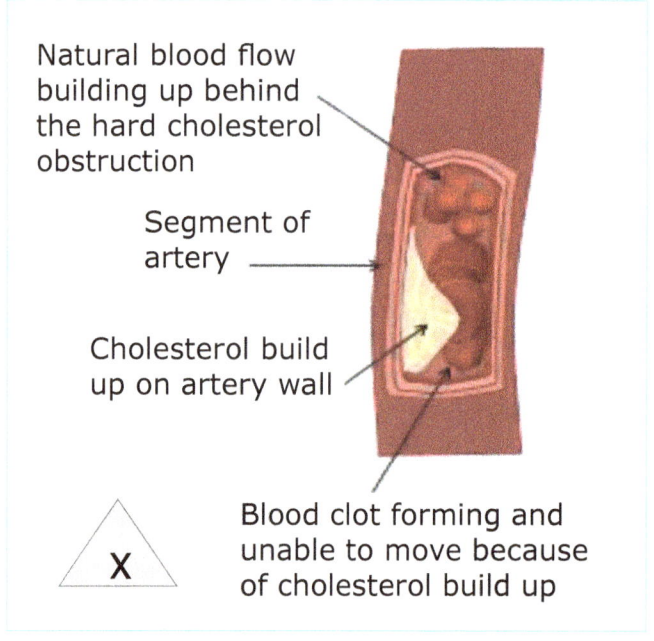

Natural blood flow building up behind the hard cholesterol obstruction

Segment of artery

Cholesterol build up on artery wall

Blood clot forming and unable to move because of cholesterol build up

The state of the artery reflects the food you eat. If you eat a constant diet of 'junk food' (a diet that doesn't contain healthy molecules), then you are guiding your body into ill health.

As seen in the above diagrams, the natural blood flow around your body will hit cholesterol walls and a backup of blood will start to accumulate. This will lead to not feeling well and health deterioration if not acted on.

IN SUMMARY

Discussing molecules as we have done is just 'the tip of the iceberg'. The subject is a unique study in biology and food science. Food science is a fascinating area which takes many years to know and understand.

With food manufacturers having little to no guidelines in place by governments, the industry is open to abuse and misuse. Putting altered molecules into the world food chain is going to lead to poor nutrition in many communities and societies. You now know the difference between a healthy molecule and an empty or dead molecule. Empty or dead molecules are in many foods sold as healthy foods worldwide.

YOUR NOTES

THE DEVIL OF SUGAR

The human brain is a magnificent piece of human technology and has taken many millions of years of evolution to get to what it is today. The brain and body are constantly changing, updating, and modifying themselves without any instruction from us. They modify and adapt to accommodate the changes needed for the species to survive.

SO, WHY IS SUGAR SUCH A DEVIL?

Little do people realise, sugar works on the brain and that is why the sugar producers and manufacturers have had a worldwide dominance since the 16th century.

Sugar is not just a sweetener; it is a poison in its refined form. Sugar also has habit forming attributes that your brain finds hard to resist.

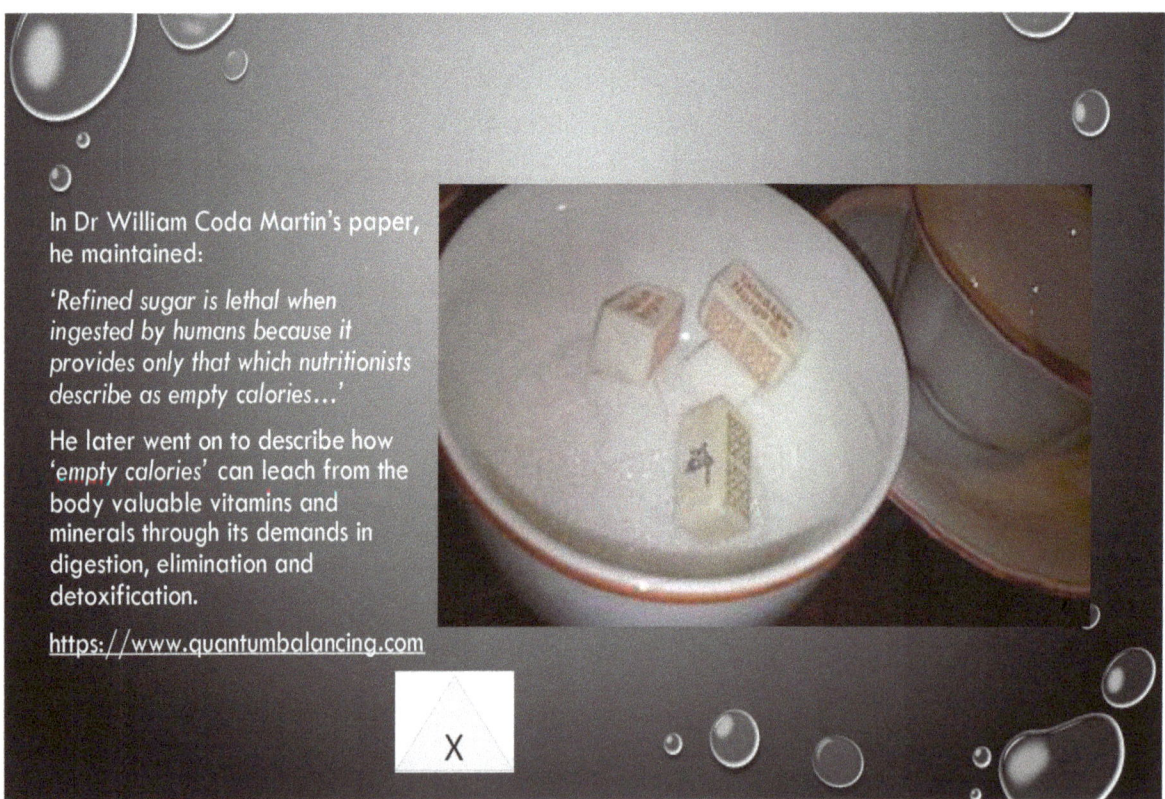

In Dr William Coda Martin's paper, he maintained:

'Refined sugar is lethal when ingested by humans because it provides only that which nutritionists describe as empty calories...'

He later went on to describe how 'empty calories' can leach from the body valuable vitamins and minerals through its demands in digestion, elimination and detoxification.

https://www.quantumbalancing.com

Sugar – A food additive – Sugar is a refined food additive; it does not carry an identification number as many manufactured additives do. However, without sugar added to food production in the global food industry, global processed food outlets would not sell their products.

THE HISTORY OF SUGAR

The original sugar cane was grown by the New Guinea natives at least 6,000 years BC. It took another thousand years for the sugar cane plant to reach other places in the world. By 5,000 BC sugar cane cultivation had spread to India, where once harvested, the sweet juice was turned into basic sugar crystals. For 400 years, sugar remained a European delicacy, spice, and luxury. The fine crystals were 'white gold' and would make many sugar merchants extremely wealthy. Christopher Columbus took sugar cane to the Americas in 1493. Sugar cane plantations were established in the West Indies and South America in the 16th and 17th Centuries. Sugar then became a vital commodity for Europe and England. In England and during the time of the Industrial Revolution and into the 19th Century, sugar intake had increased by 1,500 percent.

In the 19th Century, refined sugar was considered a necessity by the people of Great Britain, Europeans, and Americans. In the 20th Century, sugar was added to nearly every food consumed. In the 21st Century sugar is still added to cereals, breads, drinks, yogurts, health bars, juices, salad food dressings, sauces, readymade meals, frozen meals, Chinese, Indian, other Asian meals, take away meals, fast food meals and numerous other foods.

THE DEVIL OF SUGAR

THE DEVIL OF SUGAR

ORIGINALLY, THE SWEET LIQUID OF SUGAR WAS SUCKED AND CHEWED FROM THE CANE FIBRE OF THE SUGAR CANE.

THIS RICH ENERGY-GIVING FOOD, IN IT'S RAW STATE, POSSES SUCROSE, VITAMINS AND MINERALS.

Sugar has been eaten by thousands of people over thousands of years.

By 5,000BC sugar cultivation had spread to India, where once harvested, the sweet sugar was turned into sugar crystals.

In this form, monks and migrants could easily transport it to China, North America and Persia. Sugar eventually reached Europe in the 11th Century.

For 400 years sugar remained a European delicacy, spice and luxury. The fine crystals were 'white gold' and would make many sugar merchants extremely wealthy.

By the 19th Century, sugar was considered to be a necessity by the people of Great Britain, Europeans and Americas and in other countries around the world.

We are now in the 20th Century and sugar still is prominent in many foods eaten by millions of people today.

SUGAR IN ITS NATURAL STATE

Sugar in its natural form is a health food for the human body. The sweet liquid can be sucked from the stem and the fibres are chewed from the cane. In its raw state, this is a rich energy-giving food, which possesses natural sucrose, vitamins, and minerals.

ONCE PROCESSED, EXTRACTED SUGAR BECOMES A TOXIN AND POISON TO THE HUMAN BODY

Once sugar cane is harvested, and processed, the health benefits previously spoken of are removed and an empty sweet sugar crystal is left. The crystals go through a bleaching process which is the sugar product we are all familiar with and buy.

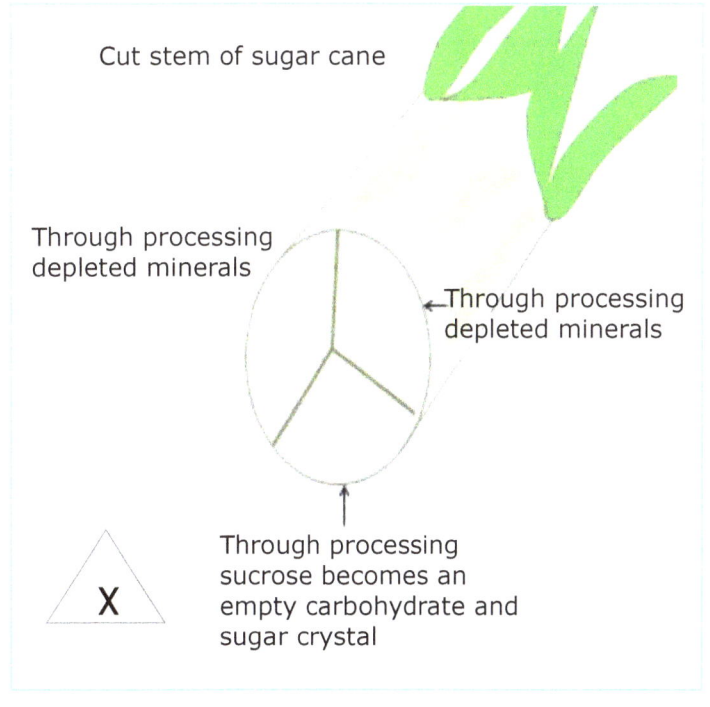

REFINED SUGAR IS A TOXIN AND POISON

Refined sugar is a toxin and poison

Added to the processed sugar are many other food additives (I will speak about food additives a little later), that allow the food to last longer (shelf life); additives can intensify the colour, add gloss, this in turn, appeals to our senses, of seeing and tasting. Once the pleasure of eating something sweet is recorded in our memories, we learn from the experience that sugar foods are nice to eat. We may not realise, they may be nice to eat, but they are indeed poison to our body's system and brain.

A sugar crystal is an empty and dead carbohydrate that offers no benefit to our well-being and individual health.

YOUR NOTES

....
....
....
....
....
....
....
....
....
....
....
....

THE LACK OF HEALTH BENEFITS WITH PROCESSED SUGAR HAVE BEEN WELL RESEARCHED

MANY CHILDREN'S FOOD PRODUCTS CONTAIN SUGAR. MANUFACTURERS INSIST ON PUTTING SUGAR AND OTHER POISONOUS SUBSTANCES INTO MANUFACTURED FOOD AND DRINKS, SO WHY IS THIS?

- **SUGAR ADDS TO MOUTHFEEL– MOUTHFEEL HELPS TO DEVELOP THE HABIT AND TASTE FOR SUGAR.**
- **A CHILD IS NOT BORN WITH THE HABIT OF EATING OR WANTING SUGARY FOOD.**
- **THE CHILD IS NOT RESPONSIBLE FOR DEVELOPING THE HABIT.**
- **ADULTS WITHIN THE CHILD'S ENVIRONMENT HELP TO CREATE THE HABIT THE CHILD DEVELOPS.**
- **SUGAR HABITS HELP LEAD TO ILL HEALTH IN YOUNG AND OLDER ADULTS.**

WHY IS SUGAR SUCH A POISON?

Natural sugar, like so many good foods, contain good food molecules. Through the processing of the sugar cane the molecules go from a health-giving food to a dead food that offers no benefit to the human body, brain, and mind.

A dead sugar molecule, like so many other dead molecules, is not recognised by the enzymes within the human gut and is therefore rejected by the gut. This lack of acceptance by the gut enzymes leads the molecule to be pushed through the intestine wall and into the human bloodstream. It now needs to park itself and this is usually done in the soft tissue of the body, usually the liver. Once the liver becomes an oversaturated, fatty liver of dead sugar molecules, the molecules need to find another parking place, this could be the thighs, once they too are saturated, the dead sugar molecules will eventually find the soft tissue of the human brain.

Creating Sweet Food Habits - When we give a baby just a taste of sweet food, we are indeed establishing the memory of the taste of the sweetness and the child will want more as it grows. Not all people gain weight after eating sugar, but processed sugar, if not removed from the body will store itself within the body. This storage could lead to gaining weight when going into and through puberty and other health conditions.

THE DEVIL OF SUGAR CONTINUES

- If statistics aren't enough….!
- In 2014/15 six million Australians aged over 18 were overweight or 36% of the community were overweight!
- Obesity results in the United Kingdom have almost quadrupled in the last 25 years
- Obesity now exceeds 35% in seven of the States in the United States, 30% in 29 States and 25% in 48 States.
- West Virginia has the highest adult rate of obesity at 38.1%

THE JOURNEY OF THE SUGAR CRYSTAL

After eating a food containing processed sugar crystals, the crystals need to travel through the human body.

The body cannot process the empty molecule and carbohydrate which the crystal has become.

When overloaded with empty sugar crystals, the body's way of coping is to store the crystals in the soft tissue of the body, usually the liver.

THE EMPTY SUGAR CRYSTAL HAS BECOME A STRAIGHT CARBOHYDRATE OFFERING NO BENEFIT TO THE HUMAN BODY OR BRAIN

In its natural state, the sugar cane offers minerals, vitamins and glucose to the human body and brain

To reiterate, like so many foods, sugar in its natural state is a healthy giving food, it is the processing of the molecule that makes the difference!

Doughnuts are not a healthy food choice option

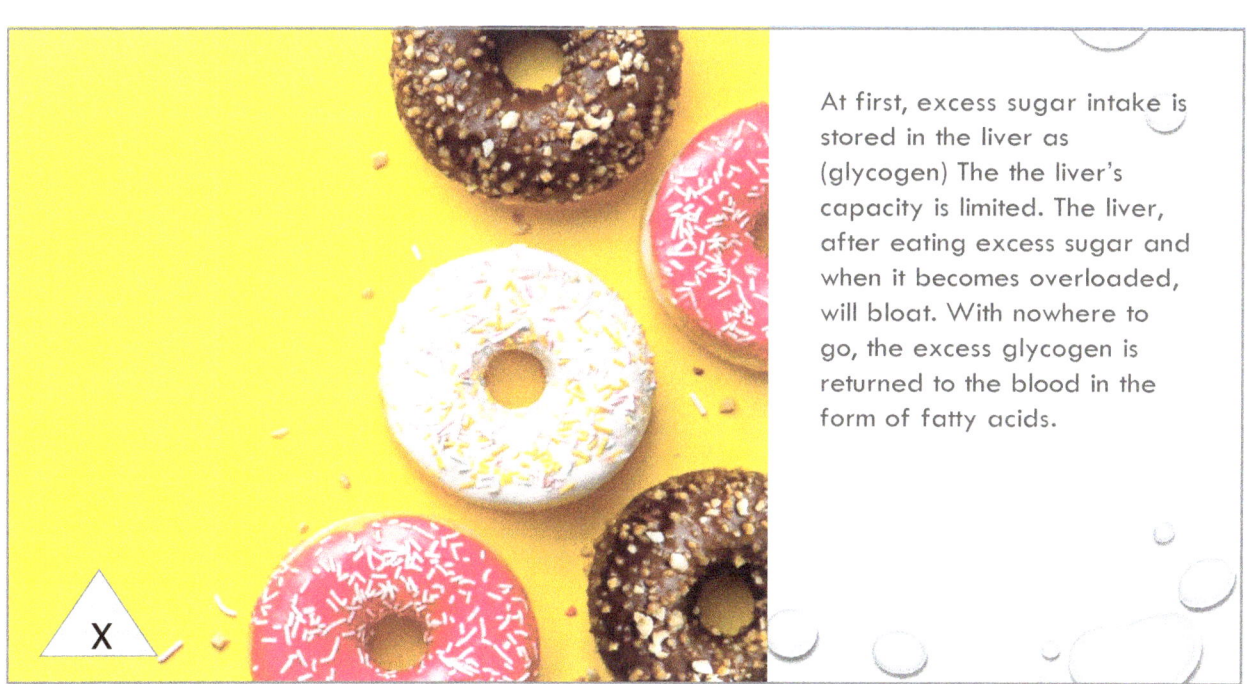

At first, excess sugar intake is stored in the liver as (glycogen) The the liver's capacity is limited. The liver, after eating excess sugar and when it becomes overloaded, will bloat. With nowhere to go, the excess glycogen is returned to the blood in the form of fatty acids.

DEFINING CARBOHYDRATES

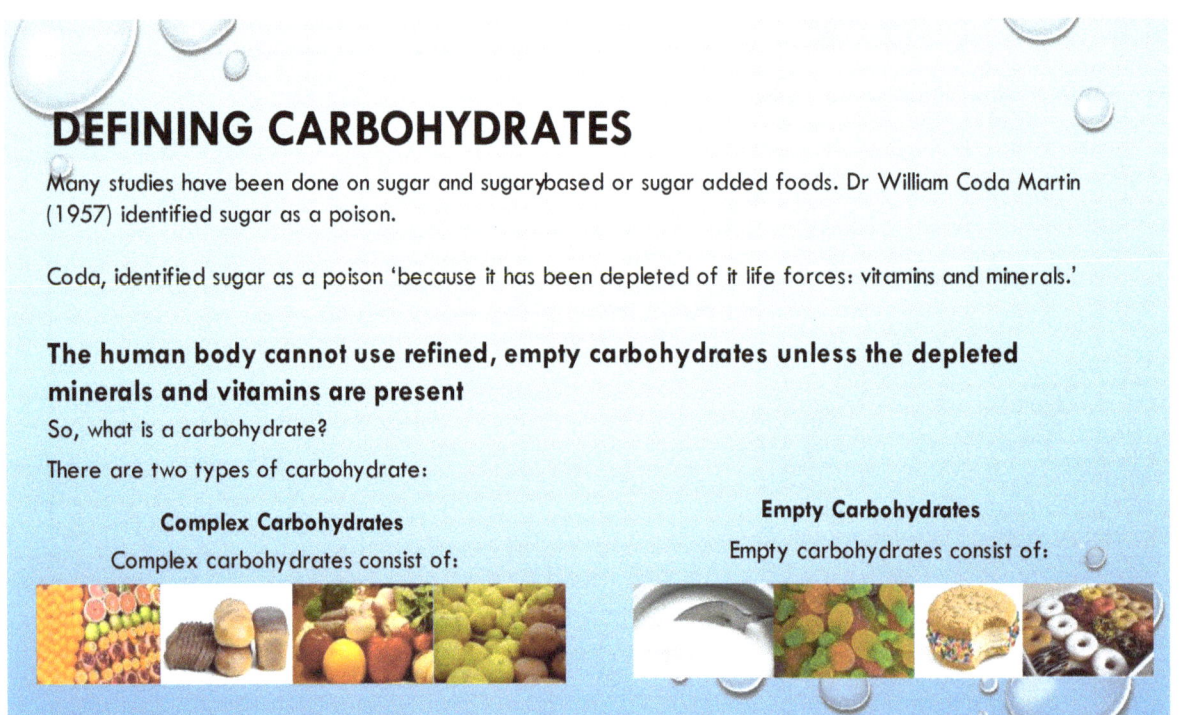

DEFINING CARBOHYDRATES

Many studies have been done on sugar and sugarybased or sugar added foods. Dr William Coda Martin (1957) identified sugar as a poison.

Coda, identified sugar as a poison 'because it has been depleted of it life forces: vitamins and minerals.'

The human body cannot use refined, empty carbohydrates unless the depleted minerals and vitamins are present

So, what is a carbohydrate?

There are two types of carbohydrate:

Complex Carbohydrates
Complex carbohydrates consist of:

Empty Carbohydrates
Empty carbohydrates consist of:

WHAT IS A COMPLEX CARBOHYDRATE?

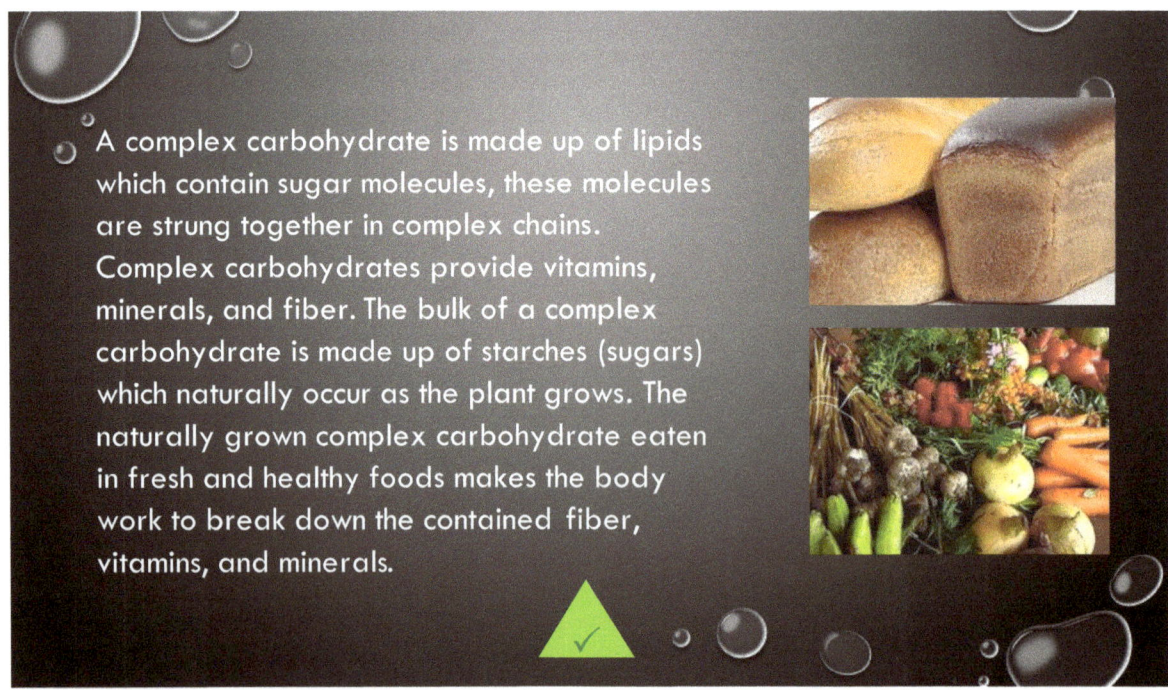

A complex carbohydrate is made up of lipids which contain sugar molecules, these molecules are strung together in complex chains. Complex carbohydrates provide vitamins, minerals, and fiber. The bulk of a complex carbohydrate is made up of starches (sugars) which naturally occur as the plant grows. The naturally grown complex carbohydrate eaten in fresh and healthy foods makes the body work to break down the contained fiber, vitamins, and minerals.

So many foods are called carbohydrate, but what kind of carbohydrate are they? There are two distinct types:

1. **Complex Carbohydrate (ALIVE, and health giving, containing healthy molecules) or**

2. **Empty Carbohydrate (DEAD, and give no health benefit to the human body, brain, or mind; they are empty molecules)**

COMPLEX CARBOHYDRATE (ALIVE MOLECULE) FOODS

Complex carbohydrates are within fresh fruit.

....

....

....

Whole, good bread made from healthy ingredients including unmodified grain.

....

....

....

Fresh, lightly cooked vegetables including pumpkin, swede, parsnip, carrots, and other natural starchy foods

....

....

....

Potatoes are high in potassium. Jacket potatoes contain highly nutritional complex carbohydrates.

....

....

....

Because the natural molecules are in place, a complex carbohydrate food has not undergone any form of processing. Your gut enzymes will recognise and accept the healthy molecules within the food you have eaten.

EMPTY CARBOHYDRATE (DEAD MOLECULE) FOODS

Many foods contain empty carbohydrate like sugar, which is within itself only a sweetener. (I have previously mentioned giving babies and young children sweet food or drinks, this could be the start of creating a bad habit for the baby or child). When, a sweet food is eaten or sweet drink is swallowed, the tastebuds inside your mouth, which connect to your brain, only recognise the sweetness. Such sweetness contributes to 'mouth feel'. Once the brain identifies the pleasure it is experiencing, it will want more and more.

Introducing you to **Mouth feel**. Mouth feel is stimulated from the 'Pleasure Centre' of your brain, otherwise known as the ventral tegmental area of the brain. Your tastebuds are connected, through your senses, (tastebuds) in your mouth by your neuron pathways which travel to your brain. The message from the sweet tasting food to your pleasure centre would resemble, 'I like that, I want to eat more of that...' and so on. This is equally the message sent to the brain when a person tries drugs or alcohol for the first time. Sugar, alcohol, and drugs are all opioids. Therefore, when some people try opioids, they find they cannot exist without the stimulant. Cigarettes, and other drugs also fall into this category. To be safe, it is better not to try any stimulant in the first place!

Worldwide, people drink annually millions of gallons of soft drink. When a soft drink is labelled 'No Added Sugar', for sweetness, many of the drink manufacturers, add harmful sweeteners. These sweeteners, because of the chemicals used in manufacturing the chemical, do as much damage to the human body, brain, and gut, as sugar.

Sweeteners, like sugar, are also empty carbohydrates. Empty carbohydrates offer your body, mind, and health nothing in return for ingesting them. Instead, they offer excess weight gain, 'brain fog' and other debilitating conditions.

Once an empty or dead carbohydrate is combined with saturated fat, (trans-fat), it offers a double-time bomb to ill health.

YOUR NOTES

UNDERSTANDING SWEETENERS

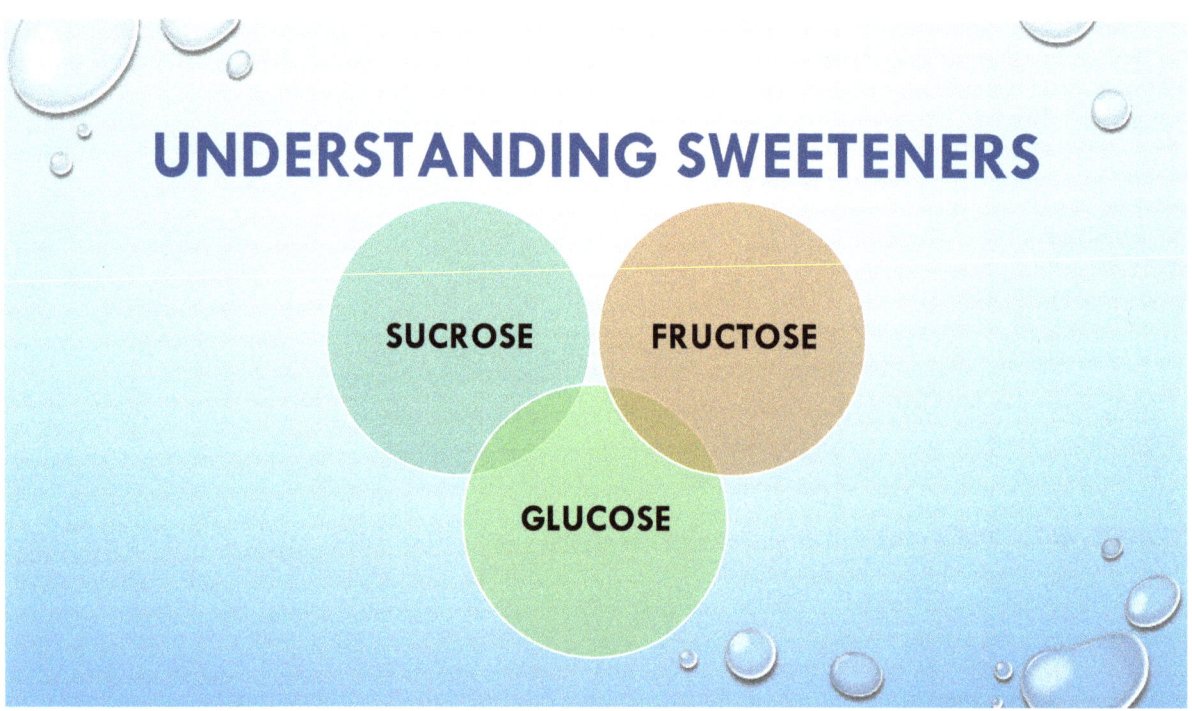

1. **Sucrose**: is obtained commercially from sugar cane and sugar beet. Sucrose is a nonreducing disaccharide. This means sucrose is made up of two carbons: glucose and fructose.
    • Sucrose should only be eaten in food or swallowed in drinks in moderation, it is an empty carbohydrate.
2. **Glucose:** Every cell in your body requires the use of glucose; glucose helps your cells to regenerate, and this helps to maintain your health. The human body doesn't need synthetic, manmade glucose, it needs the glucose it extracts from whole food in fresh fruit and vegetables.
    • Glucose comes from natural complex carbohydrates and is the food that keeps your brain healthy; its waste is recognised by your flora or gut enzymes.
3. **Fructose**: or fruit sugar is a simple ketonic monosaccharide found in many plants. When fructose and glucose carbons bond together, they produce sucrose. Ketonic monosaccharides are the simplest form of sugars.

- Fructose is the natural sugar within natural fruit; it is very good to eat but should only be eaten in moderation. Excess fructose can accumulate around the liver resulting in a 'fatty liver' condition.

Q) What is the difference between a carbohydrate and a complex carbohydrate?

Your Answer

....

....

Testing yourself

Q 1) Where would you find a (dead) carbohydrate

A) in a piece of meat? [   ]

B) in a fresh carrot? [   ]

C) in a slice of chocolate cake? [   ]

D) in a fresh fish fillet? [   ]

Q 2) Where would you find fructose?

A) in a sausage roll? [   ]

B) in a slice of orange? [   ]

C) in a vanilla slice? [   ]

D) in the orchard? [   ]

Q 3) A complex carbohydrate is found in fresh and good food

A) in a mars bar? [   ]

B) in a packet of Twisties? [   ]

C) in a banana? [   ]

D) in a sticky date pudding? [   ]

ANSWERS

A) Class discussion, Q 1) C, Q 2) B & D, Q 3) C.

BRAIN HUNGER

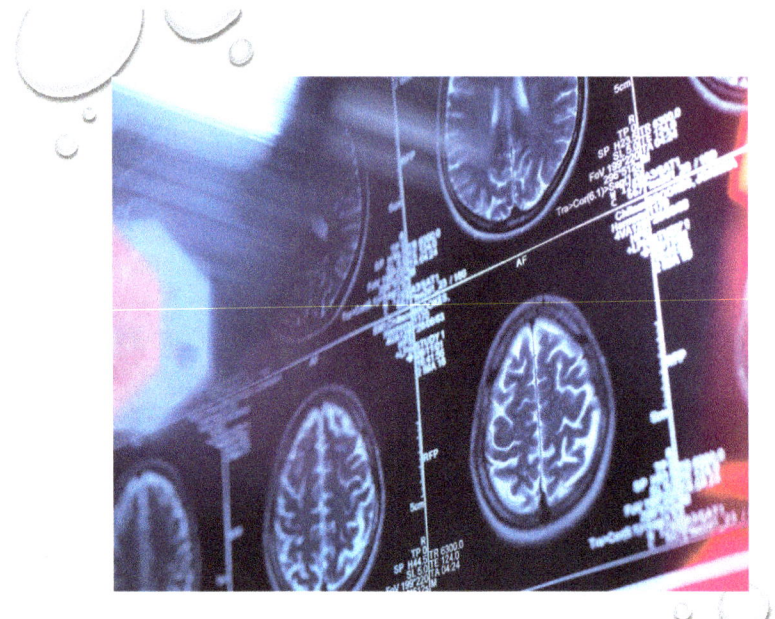

BRAIN HUNGER

Food Insecurity

Brain hunger can be linked to Food Insecurity. This situation is often found in Third-World countries. Having said that, my own research while teaching and working with young offenders in the United Kingdom, has shown that brain hunger can indeed affect the healthy growth of the young brain. Brain hunger produces lethargy, lack of commitment to any given task and difficulties in learning new concepts.

Brain hunger can reveal itself in many negative ways

Brain hunger

Brain hunger or brain starvation produces lethargy, lack of concentration and a lack of commitment to any given task. Because of a poor diet, many children and some adults suffer with 'brain hunger'. Food that has little to no value in mineral and vitamin content can produce 'brain hunger'.

Brain hunger can be caused by:
- Eating an over sugary diet as in eating large quantities of cakes that contain many forms of different sweeteners or eating excess commercially made sweet or lollies.
- Over-processed food as in many takeaway, fast-foods that can have a large sugar and trans fat content.
- Commercially made biscuits especially those with sugary and jam toppings, artificial icing and other synthetic sweeteners.
- Many commercial breads can contain large sugar and fat quantities as in rolls, brioche, rolls or buns used in take away foods and other commercially made food.

All such food and more, can contribute to Brain Hunger in Children and Adults.

Questions to ask yourself

1. Do you feel or have you been frustrated and don't know why?

2. Do you feel unwell after eating food such as takeaway meals, 'junk food', too much sugar or other non-healthy food?

3. Do you go off and become uncontrollably angry at siblings, parents, or the people you love for no reason?

4. Do you have little to no energy to do schoolwork while at school and cannot be bothered to do it at home, though you have told your teacher and parents you will?

Can you relate to any of the above?

Please write your answers below:

1. ....
....
2. ....
....
3. ....
....
4. ....
....

Extra Information for you – Case Study

A case study in the United Kingdom identifies a young male who has eaten a processed food diet over a long period of time is now classified as legally blind and deaf. Please see: Dominic Lipinski/PA Lizzie Roberts, The Telegraph UK 3/9/2019

Brain hunger can be the cause of many bad behaviours, and anger episodes.

SO, HOW CAN BRAIN HUNGER REVEAL ITSELF…?

There is usually a reason behind a child feeling angry…

Children's actions can be the result of eating too much 'junk food' or from the food they have been given to eat (often by an adult) has little to no nutritional value for the child's body or brain…

The child and adult brain uses between 65% - 75% of the food energy their food provides…

SUGAR – THE EMPTY CARBOHYDRATE, BRAIN HUNGER AND THE CHILD'S GROWING BRAIN…

Children love to learn, explore, grow and show interest. Their diet can interfere with these natural processes

Food additives, including a sugary diet and processed fats are now scientifically proven to interfere with learning, growing and child development

As an empty carbohydrate, sugar has proven to slow learning and the understanding of new concepts difficult to learn for many children

It is a natural development in all young and many older people to learn, explore and show interest. A poor diet containing dead molecules can interfere with this natural process.

SYMBIOTIC RELATIONSHIPS

Many of us take a range of vitamins every day, including vitamin B. Did you know that vitamin B is also produced in your gut? There is a symbiotic relationship that works 24/7 to keep you healthy. This very good health practise can be easily interfered with through eating over-fatty processed, over-sugared processed or manufactured foods and over-sugared drinks. Not only do the these interfere with the symbiotic relationship, but additive numbers and chemicals introduced into your body's system, through eating processed food, can also interfere with your wellbeing.

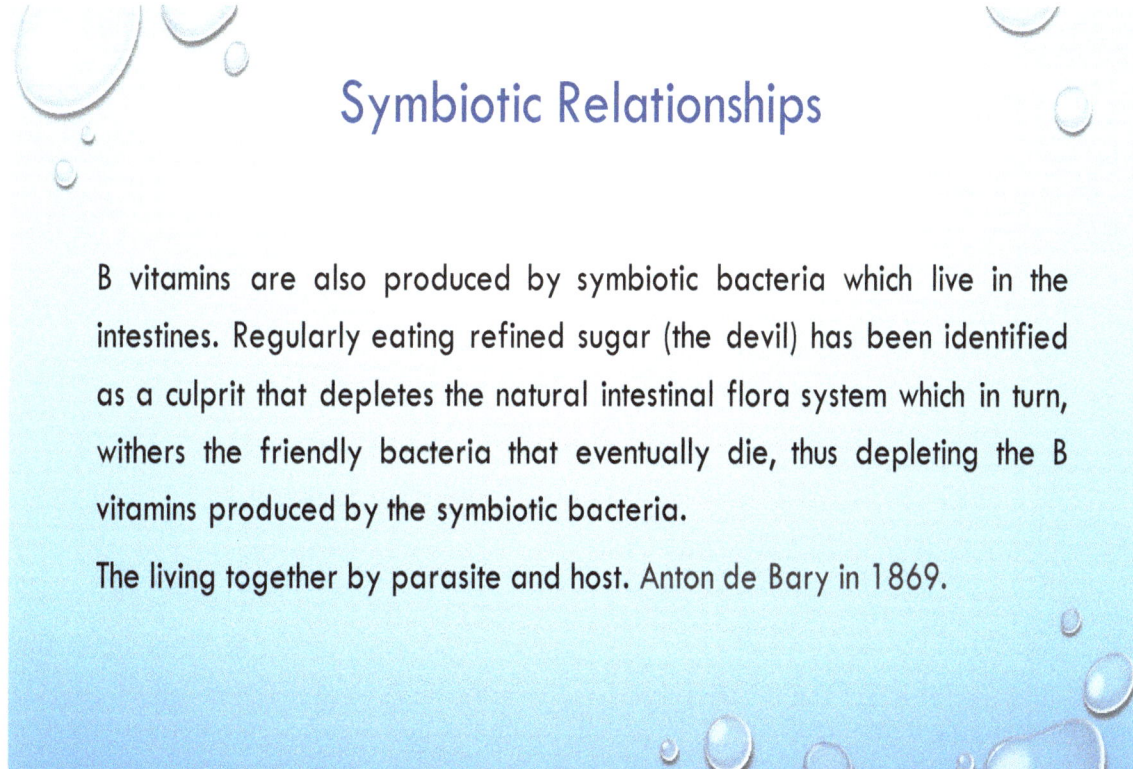

Symbiotic Relationships

B vitamins are also produced by symbiotic bacteria which live in the intestines. Regularly eating refined sugar (the devil) has been identified as a culprit that depletes the natural intestinal flora system which in turn, withers the friendly bacteria that eventually die, thus depleting the B vitamins produced by the symbiotic bacteria.

The living together by parasite and host. Anton de Bary in 1869.

An interruption in your symbiotic gut health can also been seen when unhealthy food is eaten, and the outcome is 'Brain Hunger' or when 'Food Insecurity' is an issue.

The magic of the intelligence in your body and brain is something that should be considered when you want to eat 'junk' or over-sugared, over-fat food.

Part of the brain is made up of a substance called glia. The glia formation in the brain resembles that of a walnut when the shell is removed. For the texture of glia, think, when you cut a mushroom in half, the texture will resemble cutting into the brain. This brain-like tissue has been found in parts of the gut. Between the brain and gut there are neuron connections, a bit like a mobile phone service – the brain talks to the gut and the gut talks to the brain! When the line is cut, like the mobile phone service when you lose connection, you become stranded! When this happens with your gut and brain, you become sick. (Please note, the words for the gut are sometimes called the bowel).

YOUR GUT AND BRAIN ARE IN CONSTANT COMMUNICATION WITH EACH OTHER

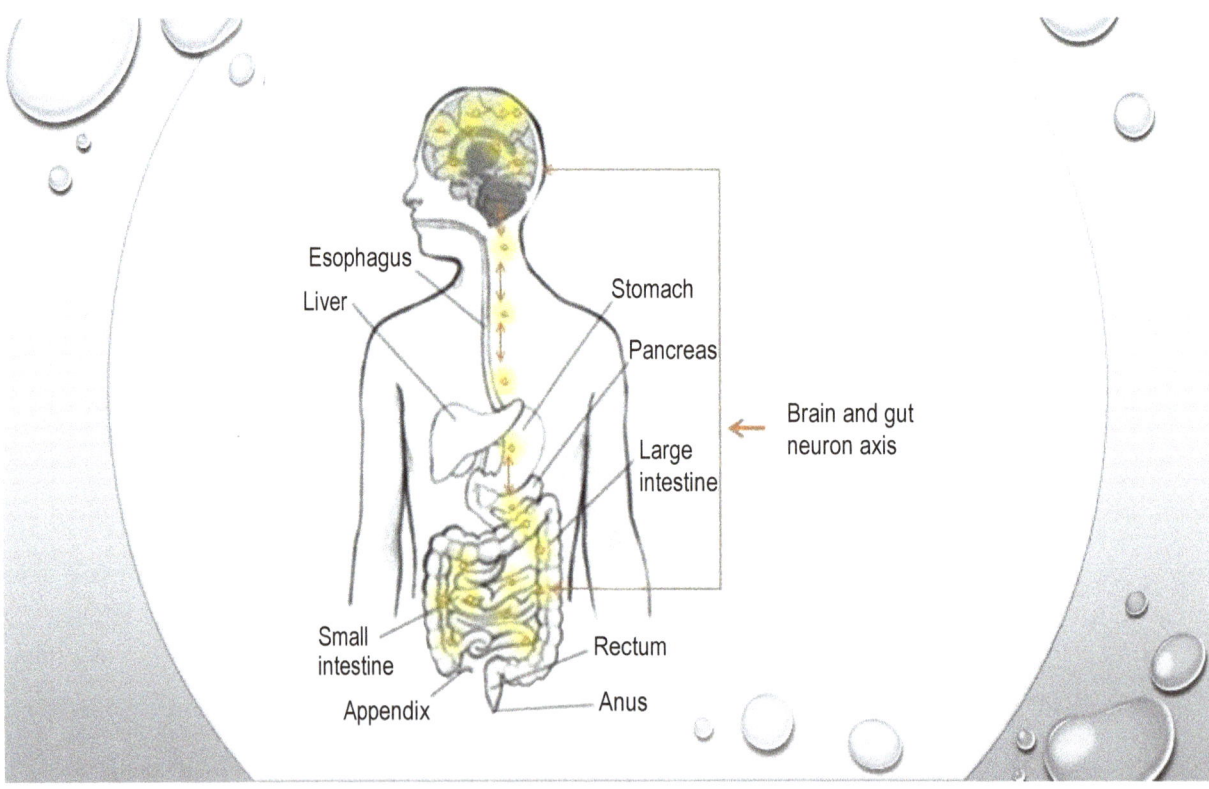

NOT ALL FOOD LABELLED AS FOOD IS GOOD TO EAT!

Some health foods, some athletic body-building food, some baby food, children's food, 'junk' takeaway food, soft drinks, including some health drinks, and more including food additive numbers, where the food is grown, how the food is processed, all lead to us eating some poisonous food at different times. This intake of poison can lead to a communication breakdown in the communication between your gut and brain! If the connection, such as when you're unable to use your mobile phone in an emergency, you are out of range, you are stuck, and it is difficult to make changes. However, with your 'brain and gut' connection, you can make instant changes and reconnect! Start by eating whole, healthy, unprocessed food!

THE MAGICAL STORY OF THE KEY AND THE LOCK - BEING SELECTIVE IN WHAT YOU EAT

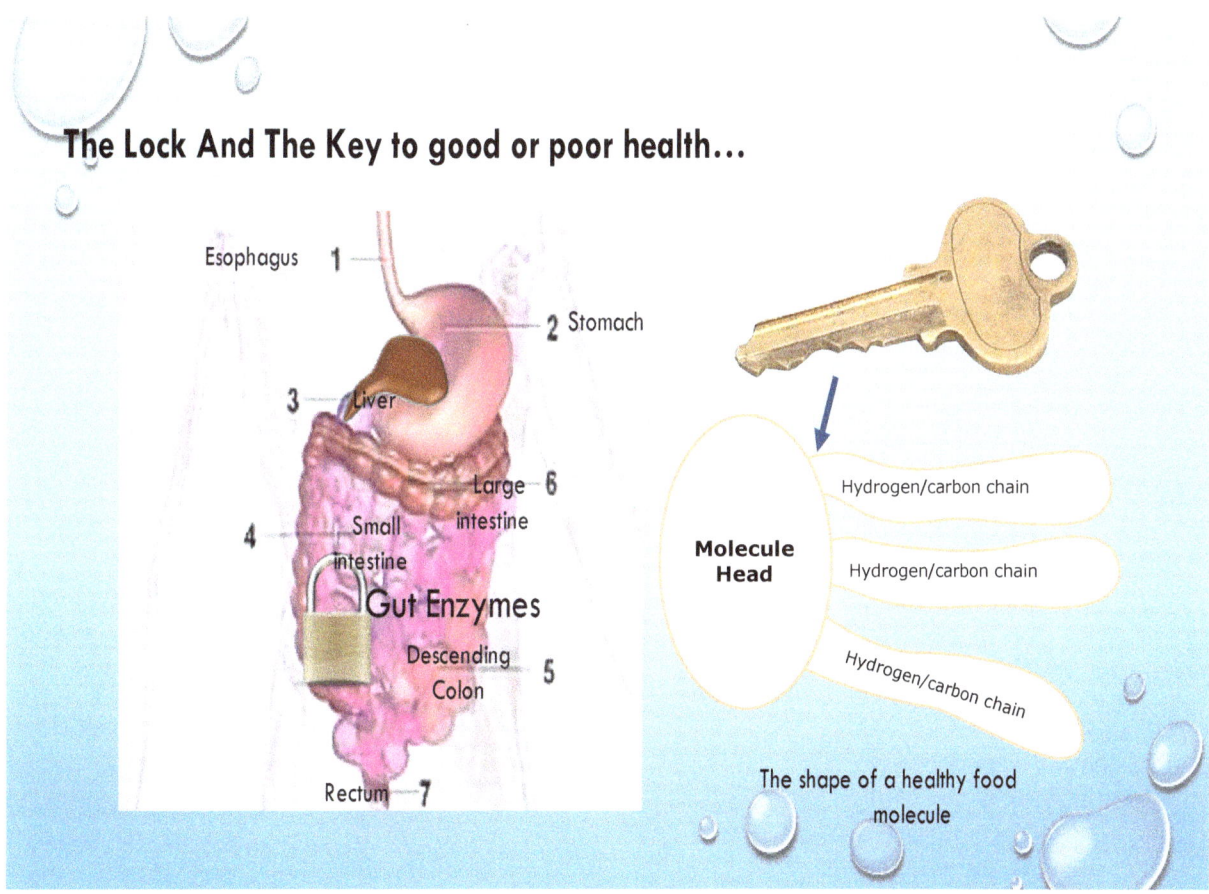

Being selective in what you eat, allows you to stay in control of the food that enters your body's system. Do you remember the story of the 'healthy' and 'dead' molecule' earlier in the lessons? This is now the continuation of a magical story.

You know now that you can eat either 'healthy' molecules that work with your body and brain to keep you healthy or you can eat 'empty' and 'dead' molecules that will contribute to poor gut health; this is your choice!

We have evolved over millions of years to be the people we are today. The original people of the world would catch and eat the food they caught. In the first instance, this was uncooked food. When our ancestors found they could cook wild food and enjoy it, that is when our brains started to become larger and higher thinking was established. These people, without realising developed,

- Cause and effect
- Stimulus and response
- Action and reaction

For instance, with the thinking, 'if I add vegetables to my meat in the pot, I will create a stew...' and so the processes of food manufacturing, though on a small scale, developed.

During this early evolution, the gut's flora developed further identifying with some naturally cooked foods, natural foods as in fruits, nuts and honey, some grasses that supply seeds used as grain and natural dairy foods from hoofed animals, including goat, beef (cow) and lamb in the form of milk and cheeses, including their meat. These foods are accepted by the gut flora, and the enzymes. Flora and enzymes are also known as the gut microbiota.

The magic of the gut key is that the lock will only accept the natural food we have evolved from. If we eat food with the wrong molecule, the KEY, the gut will not allow the food to be digested properly. It is only when the KEY, natural food and drink are consumed, does the 'KEY' fit the gut microbiota.

When you eat any form of processed food and drink, your lock and key identity will kick in. By having a key that doesn't fit the lock, you may end up with,

- Gut discomfort
- Unhealthy skin breakouts
- Poor performance in schoolwork or athletics
- 'Brain Fog' and the inability to think clearly
- Lack of interest in life
- Mood swings including anger and short-temperedness
- Depression
- Weight gain and
- In general, poor behaviour in your social and family life

CLASS DISCUSSION

Q1) Now you understand how the 'KEY' works in the food you eat, how would you explain this to your family, friends, or classmates?

....
....
....
....
....
....
....
....
....

Q2) Discuss with your family, friends or classmates, the types of food within the 'KEY' and how some foods could be locked out from entry within the gut.

....
....
....
....
....
....
....
....

YOUR NOTES

....
....
....
....
....
....
....
....
....
....
....
....
....
....
....
....
....
....

GREEN AND LEAF VEGETABLES

HELPS YOUR BODY TO BUILD THE IRON IT NEEDS THAT KEEPS YOUR BLOOD HEALTHY

GREEN FOODS HELP TO KEEP YOUR BRAIN HEALTHY

THEY HELP TO KEEP YOUR SKIN HEALTHY AND LOOKING GOOD

GREEN FOOD HELPS YOUR BONES TO STAY STRONG

THEY HELP YOUR GUT TO STAY HEALTHY AND SO YOU FEEL GOOD AND DON'T GET A STOMACHACHE

GREEN FOODS ALSO HELP TO BOOST YOUR IMMUNE SYSTEM AND WILL HELP TO KEEP YOU SAFE FROM VIRUSES LIKE COVID

Green vegetables should be freshly picked, washed then eaten. They provide a range of goodness for all parts of the body and brain, but mostly your blood; when your blood is healthy, you are healthy.

- ✓ Green foods help your body to build the iron it needs; this helps to keep your blood healthy
- ✓ Green foods help to keep your brain healthy
- ✓ Green foods help to keep your skin healthy and looking good
- ✓ Green foods help your bones to stay strong
- ✓ Green foods help your gut to stay healthy which helps to prevent stomach aches and gut discomfort
- ✓ Green foods help to build your immune system and will help to protect you if you should be attacked from a virus like Covid or the Delta variant.

Question – When did you last eat green food?

Your Answer ....

TO KEEP YOUR BLOOD HEALTHY, IT NEEDS A REGULAR SUPPLY OF FOLIC ACID

Folic acid is found in, dried beans, peas, lentils, oranges, whole-wheat products, liver, asparagus, beets, broccoli, brussels sprouts, spinach and in a range of green leafy vegetables.

YOUR NOTES

....
....
....
....
....
....
....

HEALTHY EATING COMES IN MANY DIFFERENT FOODS

Fruit and vegetables.

....
....

Starchy food including bread and potatoes.

....
....

Dairy foods including yogurt, cheese, cream and milk.

....
....

Healthy fats from some plants, as in olives, nuts, lamb, goat, and beef.

....
....

Protein including fish, meat, and eggs.

....
....

EXPANDING ON PROTEIN FOODS

Like the egg sandwich, previously spoken of in the earlier lesson; eggs are often combined with complex carbohydrates like healthy breads.

However, there is some confusion over what are healthy and unhealthy protein foods that are good to eat; we may be able to clear some of this confusion up with the following information.

EXPANDING ON HEALTHY PROTEIN FOODS

- Unprocessed meats include, lamb, beef, chicken, goat, and other whole meats including offal. These meats can be cooked at home, cut, and kept fresh in the fridge. Other foods include:
- Eggs
- Fresh fish including tuna and shrimp
- Some cheeses, including dairy foods such as whole milk, yogurt, and cream
- Some nuts including almonds and peanuts and peanut butter
- Oats
- Whole milk
- Lentils
- Broccoli and sprouts and
- Quinoa

UNHEALTHY PROTEIN FOODS

- Processed meats include ham, bacon, salami, spam, and other processed meats. Many of these meats contain artificial food colours, chemical additives including nitrites, Monosodium L-glutamate MSG (621), please see page 42, for a detailed outline of this food additive.

HEALTHIER PROTEIN FOODS

- Some healthier processed meats are now available, these do not go through modern processing using additives, chemicals, food colours, preservatives, and nitrites.

EXTRA NOTES

....
....
....
....
....
....

FOOD ADDITIVES

Within Australia, and other countries, food and drink processing and manufacturing industries, the producers must only show the food additive ingredient on the food ingredient panel of the package if the ingredient is 5% or over of the measured ingredient. If for instance, foods or drinks containing additives of 4.99%, these do not have to be shown on the ingredient panel. Therefore, many foods and drinks containing dangerous food additives of 4.99%, can be included in food and drink manufacturing without the consumer being made aware, they may be drinking or eating foods containing poisonous additives!

Food additives start at 100 and go through to 1522. In my book. Devils In Our Food, I have identified three distinct groups, these are:

SAFE **CAUTION** **AVOID**

Most additives come into the AVOID category and are unfit for human consumption. With so many, I have identified six of these in this next section. The origins of many food additives are untraceable.

Please take the time to read and discuss these additives with your classmates and friends.

104 **Avoid**	**Quinoline yellow**

Colour: Dull yellow to greenish yellow
Is an artificial coal tar dye used in the production of some food. Found in ices and ice cream, scotch eggs and smoked haddock. May cause dermatitis if used in lipstick manufacture. Is linked to cancer. Also used in hair products and colognes. Commonly used in the United Kingdom. Banned in Germany, Norway, Australia, and United States. **Avoid**

YOUR NOTES

....
....
....
....

123 **Avoid**	**Amaranth**

Colour: Purple to red (blackcurrant)
Is a synthetic azo dye derived from coal tar. Found in ice cream, jams, jelly, tinned fruit, pie fillings, trifles, prawns and in gravy granules. May cause skin rash and skin disorders. Intolerance to asthmatics and can provoke eczema and hyperactivity in some children. It may cause birth defects and has caused foetal defects in some animal testing. Possibility of a link to cancer. Not recommended for children. Banned in Russia, Austria, Norway and restricted to caviar in France and Italy. On alert in the United States. Approved in the European Union, New Zealand, and Australia. **Avoid**

YOUR NOTES

....
....
....

133 **Avoid** 🟠	**Brilliant blue FCF**

Colour: Blue powder or granules
Aluminium solution or ammonium salts. Is an artificial food colouring used to make candy floss, (cotton candy), ice cream, canned and processed peas, blueberry flavoured products, dairy products, sweets, icings for cakes, children's ice blocks, drinks, confectionary, and mouthwash. Asthmatics avoid. Suspected of being a carcinogen. Linked to hyperactivity in some children. On alert in the United States. Approved in the European Union, New Zealand, and Australia. **Avoid**

YOUR NOTES

....
....
....
....

173 **Avoid** 🟠	**Aluminium**

Colour: silver grey
There is no dietary requirement within the human body for this additive. Is used in sugar-coated and flour confectionary decorations and in the presentation of dragées (small bite-sized confectionary with a hard, external shell). May be used in other foods and drinks. Is linked to premature senility, Parkinson's and Alzheimer's disease, osteoporosis, some kidney disease, toxicity of the nervous system, cardiovascular system, the reproductive and respiratory systems. Banned in some countries. On alert in the United States. Approved in the European Union, New Zealand, and Australia. **Avoid**

YOUR NOTES

....
....
....

203 **Avoid** ●	**Calcium sorbate**

Colour: White crystalline powder
Is a chemical preservative used in jams, soft drink, meat, cider, concentrated fruit juice, dried apricots, fermented milks, frozen pizzas, fruit salads, margarine, processed and sliced cheeses, salad dressings, table olives, wine, yogurt, glacé cherries, sweets, lollies and confectionary. Contributes to ADHD. Aggravates and contributes to behavioural problems, asthma attacks and allergic reactions. Causes skin irritation, dermatitis, itching and hives. Not recommended for children. Approved in the United States. Now banned in the European Union.[2] Approved in New Zealand, and Australia. **Avoid**

YOUR NOTES

....
....
....
....

621 **Avoid** ●	**Monosodium L-glutamate or MSG**

Colour: Odourless, Crystalline Powder
Is a sodium salt from 620. A synthetic derived from molasses by bacterial fermentation. Is used in bread and bakery goods as a flavour enhancer. Used as a low-sodium salt substitute in many commercially produced food products. Is also added to any 'dead, poor or bad tasting' processed foods. Used in canned tuna, canned vegetables, sausages, cracker biscuits, instant noodles, soups, stock cubes, dressings, potato chips, pre-packed meals, snacks, and Chinese and Asian meals. Will cause headaches, dizziness, nausea, neck pain, migraine, asthma, hyperactivity, and behavioural problems including ADD, ADHD and other behavioural changes. Can be a factor in insomnia and increase appetite contributing to obesity problems. Is linked to neurological disorders including Alzheimer's, Huntington's, and Parkinson's diseases. Not suitable for babies, young children, pregnant or lactating women. A dangerous synthetic additive that should be banned. See 620. Approved in the United States, European Union, New Zealand, and Australia. **Avoid**

---

[2] https://www.foodnavigator.com

YOUR NOTES

....
....
....
....

SOFT DRINK ADDITIVES

Synthetic caffeine is used in many health drinks and health supplement foods. It's also used in a wide range of soft drinks sold in the worldwide marketplace; these are often marketed and aimed at the young adult population.

All synthetic caffeine is made in China, with little to no regulation on the materials used in the manufacture of the product. Without regulation, mistakes will happen.

In Australia and New Zealand, food and drink manufacturers have no legal requirement to state that synthetic caffeine is used in their product. By looking at the product label you will see the word caffeine – what type of caffeine will not be stated.

Many parents and teachers don't necessarily know about the young teenage adults that drink synthetic caffeine in manufactured drinks on the way to school. Of course, there is more to a synthetic caffeinated drink than just caffeine there are also the other food and colour additives to consider.

By understanding that not all food and drink additives are a health benefit; they in fact, can cause long-term ill health for you and for many people worldwide.

THE STORY OF SYNTHETIC CAFFEINE

Synthetic caffeine was first produced in 1942, during WWII, by the Nazis in Germany. Synthetic caffeine is cheap to produce and can be manufactured by unregistered producers. To produce synthetic caffeine, ammonia[3] is converted into urea, this undergoes many steps of change including exposure to methylene chloride, ethyl acetate, and carbon dioxide. When the original processing is completed, the substance glows. The glow is removed by rinsing with acetic acid, chloroform, sodium carbonate and sodium nitrite. These processes produce synthetic caffeine found in many foods and drinks available on the supermarket shelf, in roadside services, cafes, general food outlets including airports, train and coach stations, fast food take away outlets and many other retail food and convenience food stores. Synthetic caffeine is used in many health drinks and health supplement foods.

SOFT DRINKS -SYNTHETIC CAFFEINE

X

---

[3] Ammonia is a colourless gas – can be manufactured or naturally produced.

EXERCISE

For a week or longer, together with your classmates, use the information you have learnt in this short course to identify dangerous food additives, and possible unhealthy foods that are readily available in the supermarket, fast-food takeaway outlets or at convenience stores. Keep your notes and discuss at an appropriate time with your teacher and classmates. When you are discussing food at home, talk to your family and friends, and include them in the discussion.

DISCUSSION

………
………
………
………
………
………
………
………
………
………
………
………
………
………
………
………
………
………
………
………..

YOUR IMMUNE SYSTEM

The world is currently faced with the Covid Pandemic and science is trying to predict and find vaccines for any future mutations. To help our worldwide science teams, we as individuals, need to play our part in protecting ourselves, and immune systems by eating healthy foods within healthy diets. The immune system can be depleted when foods containing processed sugars, trans-fats, food additives and other poisonous food substances are used in food production, then eaten by the consumers. The Western diet, including fast food, is high in salt, sugar and trans-fat, yet low in fibre; this is no good for your gut, brain, health, and wellbeing.

In a German study, Dr. Eicke Latz witnessed changes to the immune system of mice. He firmly believes, *'…that eating a diet high in fat, sugar, and sodium, permanently alters the body. This study shows that the immune system has a memory. He says the body's response to fast food is the same as an infection. The immune system becomes aggressive. When the body is sick, the defence team goes into a panic state. It begins working in overdrive. It quickly identifies any new attacks and responds faster than usual.'* [4]

The body's response to eating 'junk food' or processed meals would suggest that not only the immune system, but the metabolism within the system is also affected by eating unhealthy food.

YOUR NOTES

....
....
....
....
....

---

[4] Junk Food Upsets the Immune System, Causing Dangerous Diseases (labiotech.eu)

YOUR RESPONSIBILITIES ARE TO LOOK AFTER YOURSELF AND TO PROTECT YOUR IMMUNE SYSTEM

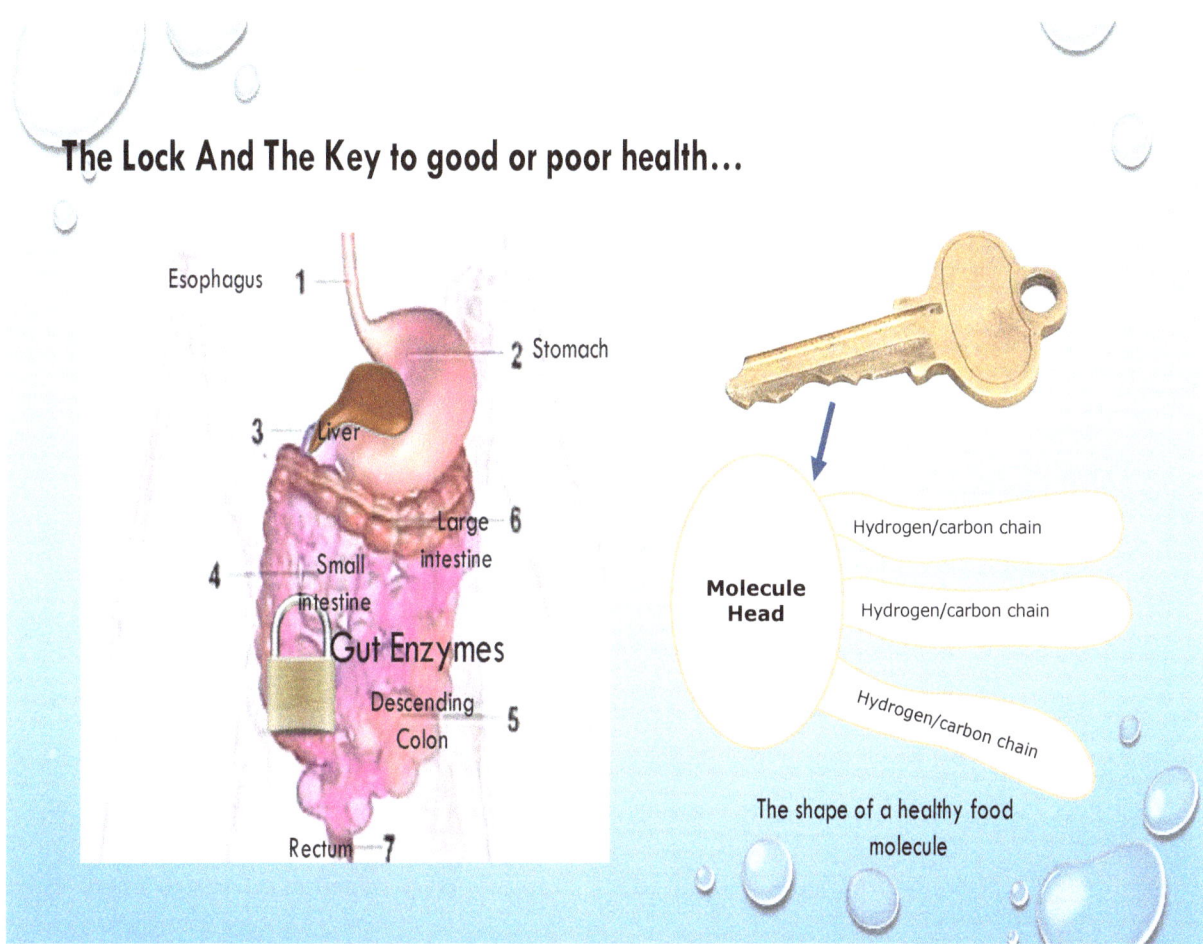

By asking, 'What is in this food?' 'How is it produced?' 'How is this food made?' 'How good is this food for me?' and other relevant questions, there will be changes for the better made to worldwide food production. These changes will relate to sustainable farming practises, which will start to regenerate farm, and pasture lands which would help to reduce global warming. Many food additives are made from the by-products of petrol and other products that cannot be identified or their origins established. By reducing food additives in produced food products, it will reduce many behaviour problems, reduce many short and long-term illnesses, and health conditions brought about by eating indigestible food.

If the above areas are not addressed and modifications made to available food, the situation of eating poisonous and non-health-giving food will become worse.

THE STORY OF THE KEY AND THE LOCK CONTINUES

With every bite of food you take, you are introducing the 'KEY', to your good or bad health. Remembering, that the enzymes in your gut flora will only accept the molecules it can identify.

At the beginning of the lessons, we spoke about feeding the masses within the world population and the Industrial Revolution. Let's now continue that story. There must be a reason why many massed produced foods are unhealthy. Trans-fat is a manmade product first developed in 1809 by Paul Sabatier a Nobel prize winner for his work in Chemistry. In 1901, Wilhelm Normann, a German chemist showed that liquid oils could be hydrogenated and patented the process in 1902. Normann's process of hydrogenation showed that whale and fish oil could be stabilised and used for human consumption. Trans-fats have been in continuous use since that time. They are continuously modified from different sources including palm and cotton oils, both of which are not accepted by the human gut flora; they are the 'wrong key to fit the gut lock.' Trans-fats are continuously used in large scale food processing and production which allows more unhealthy food to be bought and eaten by the global population.

By accepting and eating inedible food, we are indeed, adding to the wealth of many food conglomerates, but this will come at a mighty human cost.

THE PARADOX OF THE SITUATION – PALM OIL

The planet is under pressure and is suffering from Global Warming. Natural forests are being depleted to grow palm oil plants, (Elaeis guineensis and Elaeis oleifera). Plant production of palm is increasing because of the demand for palm oil by worldwide processed food manufacturers. As discussed earlier, the 'KEY' of the molecule must fit the 'LOCK' of the gut flora, if this does not happen, people develop many gut-related illnesses, diseases, and gut ill-health.

The human gut cannot accept hydrogenated palm oil products, or other hydrogenated food additives related by-products from palm oil. Simply, the key molecule of hydrogenated palm oil does not fit the human lock within the human gut.

Palm products are cheap to produce, cheaper than sugar, and allows food manufacturers to make cheaper unhealthy, non-digestible food, which sells in the worldwide community.

BIOFUEL

To make matters worse, global companies are researching the use of palm oil for use as a transport fuel for vehicles and machinery as petrol is used today. If hydrogenated palm oil is used to fuel engines, it is the same as using fossil fuels, if this is so, how will this reduce Global Warming?

A DOULBLE DISADVANTAGE TO THE PLANET AND WORLD POPULATION

Meanwhile, more natural forests will be depleted (the lungs of the earth), to grow palm. Depletion of great global areas of forest contributes to Global Warming. Hydrogenated palm oil, because of its cheapness to grow and the high demand, will continue to be used by global food manufacturers to produce vast quantities of nutritionally poor food, which will result in more human sickness within the world population; this paradox does not make sense.

FOOD INTELLIGENCE FOR YOUNG ADULTS – Your journey begins. The questions you now need to start asking of food and drink manufacturers and producers, 'What is in this food or drink?' 'How good is this food or drink for me?' and 'How is this food or drink made?'

YOUR NOTES

CLASS DISCUSSION

MARKETING

The commercial food marketplace is fickle and artificial. The youth of the world are bombarded with gimmicky, bright lights advertising usually with a celebrity or famous face that is going to help the sales figures reach new high sales targets.

Much of the marketing (or branding) targets children, young people, or young adults. The marketing campaign will have a particular message that is targeted towards a singular group. That group may be the younger population with new ice blocks for the Christmas party, or older age groups introducing a new type of alcoholic drink for a birthday or other celebration! Marketing is all about working on your emotions and values. Emotions are attached to your self-esteem, your image, your values, and your vulnerability. Such vulnerability will leave you with the feelings, (I will be left out of the crowd if I don't buy or eat this). People can be encouraged to spend vast amounts of money if they feel threatened or undervalued.

Logos Courtesy of Wiki Commons

Images seen on the opposite page are designed not only for product recognition but to increase sales.

In effective marketing of food and drink products, a subtle message can be spoken without a word being said. That is the cleverness of effective marketing. Colour, word, font size and design, also play their part in adding to the feeling of attachment we all develop when we see a brand or symbol that we identify with, and in many instances, trust.

YOUR NOTES

……
……
……
……
……
……
……
……
……
……
……
……
……
……
……
……
……
……
……
……
……

FOR TEACHERS AND PROGRAMME PROVIDERS

Meeting Curriculum Objectives
NUTRITION

FOOD INTELLIGENCE – FOR AUSTRALIA

Overview Meeting: SCOOTLE TLF ID M016338

The Australian Curriculum addresses learning about food and wellbeing in two ways:
- in content descriptions as in Health and Physical Education (HPE),
- Science and Technologies, noting that in HPE there is a food and nutrition focus area and in Design and Technologies there is a technologies context (food specialisations)

The scope of learning in food and wellbeing reflects relevant content from across the Australian Curriculum.

The Australian Curriculum Connection: Food and wellbeing provides a framework for all young Australians to understand and value the importance of good nutrition for health and wellbeing both across learning areas and specifically within the Technologies. Within the learning area as in the technology's context in the core learning across Foundation to Year 8 and as additional learning opportunities offered by states and territories in Years 9–10.

The food and wellbeing connection is presented in bands of schooling. In Foundation – Year 6, the connection is described as nutrition, health, and wellbeing. In Years 7–10, it is described as home economics.

Rationale

There are increasing community concerns about food issues, including the nutritional quality of food and the environmental impact of food manufacturing processes. Students need to understand the importance of a variety of foods, sound nutrition principles and food preparation skills when making food decisions to help better prepare them for their future lives. Students should progressively develop knowledge and understanding about the nature of food and food safety, and how to make informed and appropriate food preparation choices when experimenting with and preparing food in a sustainable manner.

The Design and Technologies food specialisations technologies context includes the application of nutrition principles (as described in Health and Physical Education) and knowledge about the characteristics and properties of food-to-food selection and preparation, and contemporary technology-related food issues.

When connecting the curriculum to plan a program of teaching and learning for nutrition, health, and wellbeing (F–6) or home economics (7–10), teachers draw on content from across the Australian Curriculum, in particular Health and Physical Education, and Design and Technologies.

Safety Consideration

In implementing projects with a focus on food, care must be taken, regarding food safety, and specific food allergies that may result in anaphylactic reactions. The Australasian Society of Clinical Immunology and Allergy has published [guidelines for prevention of anaphylaxis in schools, preschools and childcare.](#) Some states and territories have their own specific guidelines that should be followed. When state and territory curriculum authorities integrate the Australian Curriculum into local courses, they will include more specific advice on safety. For further information about relevant guidelines, contact your state or territory curriculum authority.

Dimensions

To maximise the effectiveness of any nutrition, health and wellbeing or home economics program delivered in schools, learning should be sequential. The dimensions of this learning are:

- individuals, families, and communities and
- nutrition and food specialisations.

www.ingramcontent.com/pod-product-compliance
Lightning Source LLC
Chambersburg PA
CBHW041712290426
44109CB00028B/2853